Poems
My First Year

By
E.D. Hunt

Poems My First Year

All rights reserved

Copyright 2013 E.D. Hunt

E.D.Hunt is hereby identified as the author of this work in accordance with Section 77 of the Copyright, Designs and Patents Act 1988

Astara Publications

Cover & Book design, Richard Hathaway

All rights reserved. No Part of this book may be reproduced or utilized in any form or by any means, electronic or mechanical, without permission in writing from the author.

ISBN: 978-1-300-91780-9

Table of Contents

Poems - My First Year

E.D. Hunt

Acknowledgments	5
Preface	11
Creation Unfolds	15
Step Lightly on Your Path	19
Judgement Reigns	23
A Changing of Guards	27
As You Change So Do I	31
Wrap Up	35
Seeds of Life	39
A Residence of Sorts	43
Let Go	47
Release the Cladding	51
Hide but no Seek	55
Stay, but not Forever	59
Pity is not what you seek	63
Coffee, Cake and Conversation	67
I Hold You Aloft	71

Must I Wait? 75
You Wound Me Sir! 79
A Charge but not by The Light Brigade 83
According to... 87
History's Hold 91
Counsellor Angel You Sit As One 95
Hear me 99

Acknowledgements

Sometimes it's hard to clarify what others bring to one's path. With the following it has been one of great ease. Their roles may have seemed miniscule, but there effect gargantuan. And so, I name you in no preferential order.

You William, Odin and Gabriel who have guided my words propelled from a heart that has felt pain and moments of joy. Thus putting pen to paper, not knowing there impact, but knowing of yours. And for this you have my love and gratitude; always.

Lorraine Millard. A beacon who's light will remain forever bright. You sat within my presence uncritical of thoughts that guided my actions and speech, hearing me like no other. Circumstances of my childhood and adulthood kept me mute. A declaration by you that "I had found my voice." seemed strange for I was not used to hearing it. However, our discussions remain and so will you within my heart. Bless you dearest.

Jackie Dutton. Your size belies your commanding strength and you came to my aid over years that I cannot count. You have now left a service that I have yet to leave. I am grateful for a vigilance I could not muster. And for that I thank you.

Gary Fitzgibbons. You made an analytical prognosis clearing away seeds of doubt that sprouted thoughts of ineptitude. My life bowed to societies demands of literacy, memory and its so-called gifts. Yet now I exhibit a freedom that only you gave. I thank you.

Abraham Hampton. Named after a president within a continent I have no desire to visit! The irony lies in your lineage. An American whose gift was to befriend a limey. A gift always treasured.

Neil McDonald. You volunteered a service that has yet to end. Corrections seen by you and I are held within this volume. We have yet to see whether it will speak volumes, or be silenced by readers and perhaps me. Our collaboration has yet to come to an end. I thank you.

Robin Yewell and my cousin Grace Wood. A similar role you took scrutinising these works. And for this I thank you both.

Andrea Encinas. You have taken a voice that would normally remain quiet. Frightened by its impact. It now sings in jubilation of the force that hovers above, and so below, as your force and direction enriches me weekly. May it never end. And for this I thank you.

My siblings must also be mentioned although their roles were not the norm. You are still a part of me Egbert, Richard and Julianna. And I a part of you.

Trevor Farris. Who scribed in calligraphy. Sadly, it is not within. But I thank you too.

Richard Hathaway. Who has brought this volume to a life now held within your hands. I thank you.

Richard Nice. In name and, at times, in nature. Your laughter reverberates within my head. As you smile, so do I. And for that I thank you.

Richard Symon. The first to view my works, not with the eye of criticism but one of praise. You spur me on in this endeavour. And for that I thank you.

A muse who will remain nameless, inspired my trilogy. You pried these words from my heart, that tried to meet yours, and failed. Divine Source. I am at your service and you at mine. Greet me with open arms on my return and I will do the same of you. I leave you with my last thank you knowing that you never left me, and I never left you.

Others I have failed to mention, but know of me, and I of you. I thank you.

Poems My First Year

E.D. Hunt

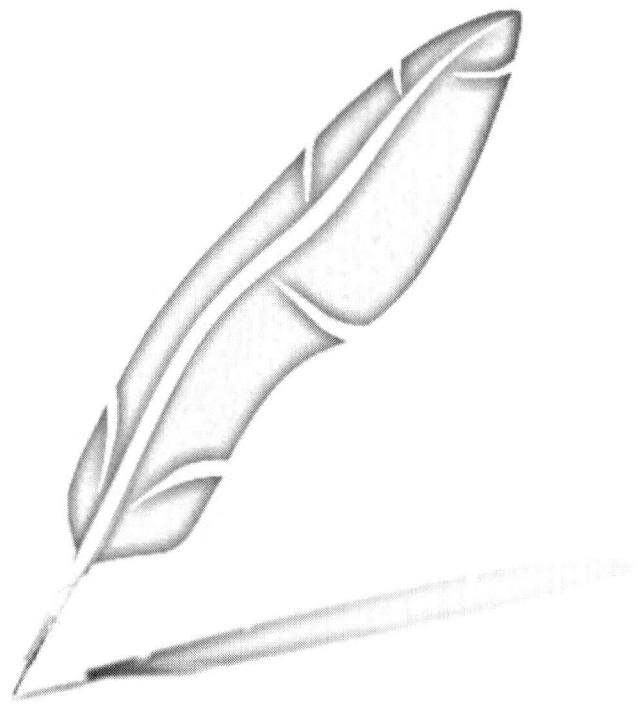

Poems My First Year

Preface

I wrote this volume in order to seek the answers to questions that we ask of ourselves. Why do we suffer through moments of anguish, pain and that of joy? Its premise is one of release, allowing anger, frustration, hurt and bewilderment to pour from my heart. I have yet to come to terms with some of life's teachings, and wonder whether I ever will.

You may well question these outpourings, as do I. When presented with life's flaws how does one express uncertainty? Are you prone to the use of words, voice or physicality to rationalise fears and seek understanding?

My words have a sincerity that I hope you feel and perhaps a recognition that you may well have faced. We are alike you and I. A nod of the head, a pondering thought seals our acceptance and knowledge of what has passed, and what is.

Poems My First Year

E.D. Hunt

Poems My First Year

Poems My First Year

Creation Unfolds

I am transfixed by a blank sheet
Yearning to be filled.
This command I will obey,
Imagination becomes reality.

Bold images dance before my eyes,
Talking to a mind that must be heard.
An outcome is secured.

Words and phrases become my weaponry
Upon the battlefield of enquiring minds.
Escaping the mundanities of life
And the release of death that will
One day take us back home.

Poems My First Year

E.D. Hunt

Poems My First Year

Step Lightly on Your Path

I stare at a future
With objects of enticement
Placed upon my path.
Their lure I succumb to,
Hoping they will grant everything I desire.

A book devoid of title holds my stare.
It lacks an author's name.
Yet to be embossed within its taut restraint
So gaining literary credence.

Housed within a corset of leather
Waits to be undone.
Disrobed by many who will read its splendour,
Marvel at its contents.
For it reveals all,
So it reveals me.

Poems My First Year

E.D. Hunt

Poems My First Year

Judgement Reigns

My inner thoughts parade themselves
Under the eye of scrutiny. Seducing the
Beholder into a world governed by
Whimsical maraudings.

Potency will either excite or enrage,
Lull or bore. Pawns pursue written perfection, pause,
and judge accordingly.

Will I be first, second, third or last?
I am first regardless of place,
Halt the slide.

I step over a threshold
Allowing imaginings to come to life, coming to all. For
I do write and compete in an
Arena that shows my living works.

Poems My First Year

E.D. Hunt

Poems My First Year

A Changing of Guards

I watch in earnest
Witnessing the birth of a new format,
Spelling the demise of a medium
Renowned for its unsurpassed power.
Two combatants sit side-by-side
Confined to a vehicle of sporadic speeds
Ferrying commuters daily.

They both hold their weapons of choice.
Clearly, one ponders its efficiency.
No force is required to draw the observer in,
Yet, the other turns leaves.
Gentle is the approach which must be read.
A rustle reinforces its closure
Folding shut.

Dog-eared corners become intertwined,
Quietly protesting the supersession
By a model whose illumination comes not from the page, but from a screen.
The e-book has left its mark.

Poems My First Year

E.D. Hunt

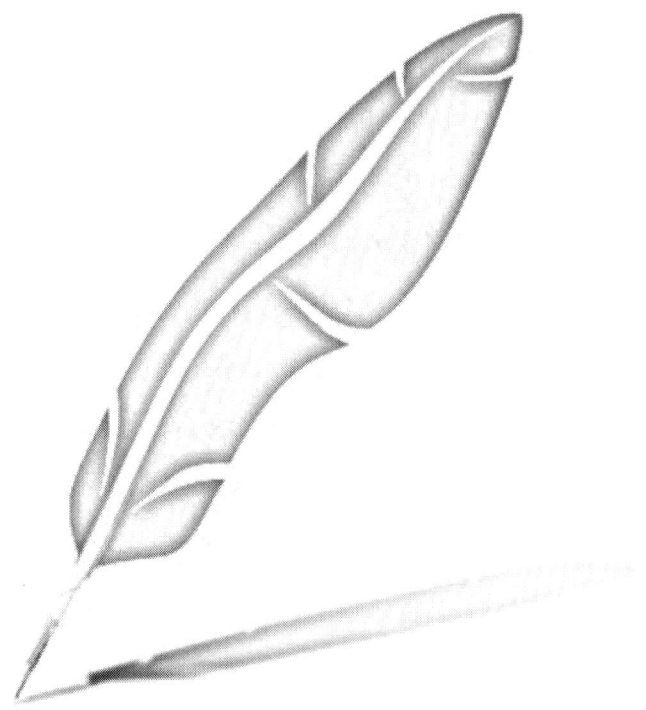

Poems My First Year

As You Change So Do I

I look for sunshine within a place that holds none.
Seasonal changes
reign.
Light and dark vie for space at an allotted time,
seemingly far too short.
Skies cover us, we in turn cover ourselves.

Attire becomes a form of defence,
Woollens shield us from elements sent from above.
Seasonal radiance halted,
Bright attitudes brought down.

Disappearing under dying light,
Hardened exteriors gain hold,
In a place that yearns for summer's rejuvenating return,
Bringing the gift of light.

Poems My First Year

E.D. Hunt

Poems My First Year

Wrap Up

Debris falls about me fluttering to the ground
weaving a carpet.
An organism living no more.
Leaves hang no longer upon the arms of branches
suspended within the air.

Their purpose has been served and lost
Under skies that draw curtains to a close.
Days grow shorter, nights grow longer.

This I see and feel,
My curtains descending over sunshine rays
That vie for existence,
In a world dominated by a change of season thus
changing me.

We are inexplicably linked, the weather and I, bound
by changes of season. Hastily Becoming one and then
become none, we disappear.

Poems My First Year

E.D. Hunt

Poems My First Year

Seeds of Life

The colours black, orange, beige and yellow invade my vision teased eyes.
Rapid vertical flights outpace individuality. Feathered friends become foes.

Physically fused body parts wings, beaks, talons show their worth.
Vocal expression erupts forth,
This melee will not be silenced and calmed.

Claiming a seed prize
A single winner from the charm.
Within your beak, Finch,
Golden in name but not in colour.

Poems My First Year

E.D. Hunt

Poems My First Year

A Residence of Sorts

I reside within this city under protest
Tethered by a force so strong,
It has me whimpering,
A ferocious cradling that has yet to recede,
Keeps me tied.

This I duly submit to,
Knowing no other choice can be made.
I continue to face the daunting days,
Becoming years,
From which I wish to forge an escape.

But my route is blocked,
Prolonged incarceration seals my fate.
My captor toys with its offspring
In an effort to reinforce dominance
Of Mother over Child.

For my crime was my place of birth,
And my sentence remains littered with objects of the greatest magnitude.

For, as St Mary's Axe falls,
So does my head.

E.D. Hunt

Poems My First Year

Let Go

I tread gently around objects
That require my presence.
Acquisitions obtained
Through sheer diligence.

Creating a fortitude that shields me
From the world of knowns and unknowns.
Their ranks swell in an effort to increase an army
governing insecurities of a troubled Mind.

Expandability is a must,
Bringing comfort to a past that saw none.
A reversal must be made, this tide stemmed.
Coexisting forms continue to dominate
The world of clutter and thus dominate me.

Poems My First Year

E.D. Hunt

Poems My First Year

Release the Cladding

Today I stare at my armour,
Wondering whether or not
It will serve me on this day.
I applaud its diligence,
The ever impregnable shell
That I deserve and must have.

I seek internal guidance,
Thoughts worthy of rebellion ricochet
Through the confines of my head;
Cradled in cupped hands, but quelled.
For notions of exposure do not suit me.

On a day that allows
The shedding of layers
And perhaps the shedding of self,
I disrobe.

Poems My First Year

E.D. Hunt

Poems My First Year

Hide, but no Seek

I am on public view,
and yet I am not.
I shroud myself in garments that
denounced my figure.
Armour is clad about my body, as I gallantly
fight the world
and its co-conspirators.

In a bid to reinforce my invisibility.
For, if I do not see myself,
how can they see me?
My disguise is foolproof!

Poems My First Year

E.D. Hunt

Poems My First Year

E.D. Hunt

Stay, but not Forever

We walked together not as lovers but as companions.
My arm intertwined within a restraint that holds you near,
Yet allows you freedom to roam in search of a world.

You smell, look at and hear a cornucopia of stimuli forcing investigation. These you
Do not rush to meet,
Backward glances request freedom.

A click sounds your release, collar and lead part.
Your search begins.
I stare at you happy in thought.

You frolic through shards of green;
Submerge yourself in the realm of nature's bounty.
From decomposition dark in colour.
Earth its name sustaining all of life
And cradling all in death.

This you probe, your nose wet, you are well.

Registering many, acknowledging all,
You give and receive attention
By the stroke of a hand,
The touch of your coat.

I continue to walk alone, now you do too.
We separated at a crossroads
That beckoned your spirit.
You returned to a home that led skywards.
I returned to a home that used to house Man's best friend.

E.D. Hunt

Poems My First Year

Pity is not what you seek

You greet me in a familiar fashion,
Illuminating, your face shows a shield of white.
Broad is your smile,
Without hesitation I am drawn to you.

Tales of woe that you must tell, leave no scars.
Buoyancy permeates you and all
Around.
Circumstances leave you seeking refuge in an iron garage.
Horses corralled under bonnets released with a key.
Destitution takes you by the hand.
My hand I extend to you. We shake.
You stand before me unhindered by this plight your life.
Saddened by your tale of woe and the home I can not share.

Poems My First Year

E.D. Hunt

Poems My First Year

Coffee, Cake and Conversation

A sound of thunder greets my ears
That do not expect it so,
A wall of solitude begins to erode.

Defence jars my body recoiling from him.
Forcing his way into my life,
Permission not sought?
His presence brings opportunities long forgotten.
For I have dined alone.

Banished for one evening, my fears quelled.
With gifts of coffee, cake and conversation
Allowing me to bask in the presence of another.
And he too basks in the presence of me.

# Poems My First Year

E.D. Hunt

Poems My First Year

I Hold You Aloft

Words that I speak will never reach your ears.
I cannot avert my eyes,
Nor do I wish to,
For I stare at a trophy set before me.
Bulk looming over me,
Reaching forward, in an effort to make it my own.

Hands glide over its surface,
Embracing every curve
Savouring that which I hold before me.
I have waited far too long
To reclaim this prize.
And I will not relinquish my grip.
For as I hold on to him,
He holds on to me.

Poems My First Year

E.D. Hunt

Poems My First Year

Must I Wait?

I immortalise you
In a fashion that only I know how,
Putting pen to paper
Allowing the yearnings of my heart
To spill forth.

I beckon and call
In the hope of being heard.
Daylight dreams allowing
Glimpses of what may be,
Make poor substitutes for reality.

Patience and a knowing
Restrain me.
His queue recedes, I remain.
To make a bond
Extended over time.

For you shall be mine,
And I yours.
Two souls become one.

Joined forever by bands of gold.
That bind proudly our hands.

E.D. Hunt

Poems My First Year

You Wound Me Sir!

I have allowed penetration of an organ,
With a weapon used in love and war.
Its aim is true and its damage unyielding,
Tears through this vessel beating with life,
That is my heart.

This arrow that you released I have caught, pierces deep.
I swerve the thrusts and parries of a life embroiled with loss.
You seek to exit our friendship
That would have you share my bed,
But not my heart.

I weep at your departure, knowing what you seek you will not obtain, you will return.
Higher forces steer you towards a path
That you fail to see, but will gain from.
I await your return, in a future bound by a ring of gold,
And a beating heart that will never still.

Poems My First Year

E.D. Hunt

Poems My First Year

E.D. Hunt

A Charge but not by The Light Brigade

I sit within a row that extends to the left and to the right placing me at its centre.
As I watch an army small in number but powerful in force wielding its weaponry,
With a grace obtained from centuries past,
Striking not foes but chords.

Strung upon instruments nestled under chins and straddled between liveried legs.
Black in colour interspersed with white, shirts drape bodies and ties make bows
Forming a circumference around the necks of men, but not of women.

All are seated around guidance that comes in human form clasping a stick that they
Must follow. Uniformity reigns upon the notes you make.
Maestro Chailly leads your charge and you, Leipzig Gewandhaus Orchestra, follow.
As Beethoven dares to look on.

Poems My First Year

E.D. Hunt

Poems My First Year

According to...

My body becomes a willing vessel
Drawn to a musical heritage depicting lives
Of pure misery.
Tarnishing many continents, many centuries,
And still to this day.

A release was sought and freedom was gained
In melodies sung with passion.
Shackles kept them bound to owners
Who showed their wealth, not their hearts.

Slaves pleading under the watchful eye
Of a creator whose presence serves all.
Their voices united in praise and that of pain. Within
this gospel cometh
Matthew, Mark, Luke and John.
And so the song.

Poems My First Year

E.D. Hunt

Poems My First Year

E.D. Hunt

History's Hold

We toiled under a Labour that kept us
bound to men who saw us as not.
Commodities sold to a bidder. Who had
us working a land that gave him wealth.
The finest clothes adorned him. Ours
 came as rags. Rings accentuated fingers.
Holding us tightly to his fold.
Our jewellery came as bangles, made not of
gold, but that of iron. Shackled around
wrists and ankles, that denoted who we were.
Slaves upon his land.

Our bangles no longer adorned our
wrists and ankles. Chains that dangled between
them and us silenced. We are not. We sing
and dance in jubilation. Gaining a right
that we longingly sought.
We are free!

Our history hardened our lives, but not our
hearts. Its tenderness we share. Bestowed

upon the young and old. Generations
apart, and yet bound by a need to nurture
you, the younger, in positions that will see
you lead. Forging communities,
flourishing under guidance you made
swayed in love.

We kneel, no longer in bondage but one of
servitude. Before an altar spreading far
and wide. Anointment touches foreheads.
Water descending downwards. Our souls
ascending skywards. That will one day
take us home. Grateful are we Father. We
your children, who sing your praises
bound in thanks. Hold no limits that you
placed upon us. And we never upon you.
I your child, giving merit to a history
decreeing a lineage that maketh me in your
image, that many see.

E.D. Hunt

Poems My First Year

E.D. Hunt

Counsellor Angel You Sit As One

I have entered this world the last of four
On a journey that has left me grazed.
Licking wounds that do not heal,
Open to the infections of life.

Rampant sores, potent, unforgiving, eclipse these eyes that seek a lighter hue.
In a world governed by experiences that hold no gain, they continue to maim me.

Questioning a sky. It's ruler labelled by religion, and thus me. Mighty are you Lord!
An earthly Guardian you have sent,
Works in tandem with you,
Bears appendages covered in feathers that only I do see.
Ministering words that
Explain my path.
Human in form and gold aura. An angel resides within.

Poems My First Year

E.D. Hunt

Poems My First Year

Hear me!

I speak to you in times of anguish,
Facing a mountain many would climb in fun
But not in haste as footing would fail.

You aid me, frequently, according to need.
As I question a path and a role that precedes me,
aiding all about me, in ways I fail to
See.
In a world that must see.

Evidence is sought and faith is gained in the dualities
of a heaven and an earth
Dominating lives. I seek to bond to your divinity in
life and in death.
I will return home, from whence I came,
Which you would not have me do again.

Poems My First Year

'Thank you for allowing me to share these works, and the time you have allocated to reading them'

Please visit my website: www.edhunt.co.uk